# LEADING THE WAY:

## *Stories of Inspiration and Leadership*

### VOLUME 5

#### Contributing Authors
Louis Vitiello, Jr.
Karen Alexander
Neal Robert Anderson, J.D.
Dexter L. Scott
Jean A. Sturgill
Dauv Evans, Ph.D.

*Foreword by Dr. Kevin C. Snyder*

Edited By Michelle Honeycutt

# Copyright 2013 © by Inspir-Active Solutions

All rights reserved. No part of this publication may be used or reproduced, stored in a retrieval system, or transferred in any form by any means, except in brief quotations in a review, without the express written consent of the individual author(s) and editor. All quotes contained within this book are written by the author(s) unless credit is specifically given to another source.

ISBN-13: 978-1494800826
ISBN-10: 1494800829

Library of Congress Cataloging-in-Publication Data:
Snyder, Kevin Charles.
Leading the Way: Stories of Inspiration and Leadership, Volume 5

1) Motivational and Inspirational
   SEL021000
2) Personal Growth
   SEL031000
3) Leadership
   EDU032000

Layout and Design by Inspir-Active Solutions and its associates.
Cover design by Byron Corporation.
Editing by Michelle Honeycutt.

For additional information, view each author's biography following each chapter and/or contact:
Email:   Kevin@InspirActiveSolutions.com
Web:     www.InspirActiveSolutions.com

To learn more about the 'Leading the Way' book series and/or to submit a chapter for consideration in an upcoming issue, please contact:
Kevin@InspirActiveSolutions.com

# Contents

Chapter 1
Louis Vitiello, Jr.
*'The Fear of Change'*

Chapter 2
Karen Alexander
*'Through The Eyes of a Child'*

Chapter 3
Neal Robert Anderson, J.D.
*'The Answer Lies Behind The Next Door'*

Chapter 4
Dexter L. Scott
*'Step Out of Mediocrity and Into Your Greatness!'*

Chapter 5
Jean A. Sturgill
*'The Crossroads'*

Chapter 6
Dauv Evans, Ph.D.
*'My BIG Promotion:
Finding Opportunities Hidden Behind Life's Challenges'*

Closing Thoughts
Kevin C. Snyder, Ed.D.

Submit a Chapter For a Future Book
About The Authors

# LEADING THE WAY:

*Stories of Inspiration and Leadership*

---

## Volume 5

Contributing Authors
Louis Vitiello, Jr.
Karen Alexander
Neal Anderson, J.D.
Dexter L. Scott
Jean A. Sturgill
Dauv Evans, Ph.D.

*Foreword by Dr. Kevin C. Snyder*

**Edited By Michelle Honeycutt**

# Introduction

*Leading The Way: Stories of Inspiration and Leadership* is a collection of leadership lessons and inspirational true stories from experts in the field of motivation and leadership, executive coaching, health and wellness, change management, and communication strategy. We have assimilated these chapters to address a variety of dynamic topics that are practical, intentional, and purposeful for impacting positive change and growth in any arena of life. By taking a few moments to read this content, the lens at which you look at life and your attitude toward obstacles will forever be changed.

These authors bring to you a richly diverse background of personal leadership experiences. The life lessons they share arise from authentic trials and tribulations over the years that have gleaned them tremendous wisdom and perspective. Their stories are like none other because quite simply, their struggles have developed their strengths. They have taken considerable time to share what they have learned through these genuine 'teachable moments' of life to help you in your quest to succeed and make a difference. Let me introduce to you our contributing authors:

**Louis Vitiello, Jr.**

Louis is an Integrative Health Coach, Motivational Speaker, and 'just a guy who lost over 200 pounds.' His business, Simple Steps Weight Loss, specializes in a unique approach to health and wellness that blends his personal experience combined with his education from the Institute of Integrative Nutrition into a fun, flexible, and rewarding program.

### Karen Alexander

Karen is a Senior Professional in Human Resources with over twenty years of experience primarily in the healthcare field. She earned her bachelor's degree in Business Administration from Charleston Southern University with a dual major in both Management and Economics and an MBA from Wingate University.

### Neal Robert Anderson, J.D.

Neal is an inspirational speaker, consultant and performance coach with a passion for helping individuals and companies increase significance and profitability. Neal is an expert at getting to the emotional difference that people make in other people's lives, and has designed retreats that get people out of the office and on a sailboat or the Appalachian Trail, the Adirondack Mountains, or the Intracoastal Waterway. His clients include everyone from a 2-time Super Bowl Champion to hundreds of top-producing sales leaders across the country. Neal earned an undergraduate degree from Indiana University, where he studied under Hall of Fame Coach Bobby Knight, and received a law degree from Vermont Law School.

### Dexter L. Scott

Dexter is the Head of Admissions for *People to People Ambassador Programs* for the states of Maryland, North Carolina, Virginia, West Virginia and the Washington, D.C. area. He works with over 2,000 families and over 200 teacher leaders each year presenting programs that take students to all seven(7) continents. Dexter has spoken to more than 20,000 people in the last three years, both nationally and internationally, in Australia, New Zealand and Europe.

### Jean Sturgill

Jean A. Sturgill speaks to both the Christian and the secular market. Her seminars and workshops focus on a range of topics from leadership, management, and business ethics to growing your relationship with the Lord. Jean is the author of multiple books, and her writing has been published in *Alamance Magazine*.

### Dr. Dauv Evans

Dauv is the Founder of Keen Advisors, LLC which specializes in personal and professional development. His background is in higher education and corporate training. Dauv earned a Ph.D. in Leadership in Higher Education from Capella University. He also holds an MBA from University of Phoenix and a B.A. in History from the University of North Carolina at Greensboro. He also teaches undergraduate business and U.S History.

As you read this book, open your mind to absorb and understand the true meaning of these experiences, successes, failures, and hardships experienced by the authors. 'Success leaves clues' and mistakes should be considered lessons of wisdom. Nothing has meaning except the meaning we give it.

Each of the following stories captures an authentic essence and philosophy of leadership that has the potential to catapult your success. However, for these accomplishments to manifest, you have to be intentional about having high expectations from this book and be willing to work diligently. As I say when I begin every keynote speech, "Life has a tendency to live up to the expectations we have for it." So 'expect' to be empowered, transformed, and enlightened about various leadership topics that will change your life in every way.

Thank you for investing time to read *Leading The Way: Stories of Inspiration and Leadership!*

**To Your Continued Success**,

Dr. Kevin Snyder
Co-Editor, Motivational Speaker, Author & Passion Enthusiast
Kevin@InspirActiveSolutions.com

*"Life has a tendency to live up*
*to the expectations we have for it."*

# THE FEAR OF CHANGE

*by Louis Vitiello, Jr.*

*"When the fear of not doing something exceeds the fear of doing it, you have no choice but to get it done."*
~ Louis Vitiello, Jr.

FEAR.

I always considered fear a funny word. In and of itself, fear is a concept that doesn't make sense. What doesn't make sense is why we allow fear in our lives. Fear prohibits us from doing the things that we most want to do. It creates challenges, blocks, and barriers. Most people stop dead in their tracks when it comes to the concept and idea of fear. Think about it, how many people do you know in your life that want to change careers, get out of a relationship, or need to have a conversation with somebody yet never do? Why don't they?

Fear stops them. It's this concept of fear that makes me believe that fear is a funny word. Not that it's spelled funny or looks funny, but a word that can create funny, questionable behavior.

Fear is a four letter word. If you believe what your mother always said about four letter words, fear being one, we should avoid them at all cost. That is the reason why people avoid a diet since that is also a four letter word. That's a different subject we will get to in a moment.

The problem I have with fear is that it stops us from achievement and growth. Think about the moments we've overcome barriers, challenges, and road blocks by doing what we were scared and fearful to do. As a result, we experienced life-long, self-gratification, happiness and achievement. Our spirit, our energy, and emotions went through the roof. We felt great about ourselves. We felt like we could conquer the world. The weight on our back was, and is, removed because we did what we were fearful of doing. We didn't before because fear stopped us.

You see this all the time: people are engaged every day and before the man proposes to the woman, or the woman proposes to the man, there is definitely a level of fear. What if they say no? The first time a singer takes the stage and opens up their voice into a microphone, there is fear. Then that artist becomes top on the Billboard's list, tours the world, and gets all the fame they'd ever imaged.

Fear.

The corporate executives, presidents, vice presidents, the tops of every major company in the world have experienced fear. No matter how comfortable they are now, their initial days were filled with fear. Even the average worker, who's just trying to make an additional fifty cents an hour, has fear when they go speak with their boss. And who knows, when they finally muster up the courage to go do it they might just get more than what they were asking for.

Fear.

For me, I had the fear of being healthy. I know that it sounds silly right now, but for me I avoided being healthy all my life. This is not to say that before I ballooned to 398 pounds that I did not try different diets to get healthy, I did. I tried a lot of different diets, a wide variety of them, and failed every time to the point that I just gave up. I got scared. I got tired of being viewed differently. I got tired of being picked on when the diets failed. I got tired of smart remarks when I couldn't lose the weight. I got tired of telling everybody that I was starting a journey to get healthier and then later have to tell them, again, that it just was not working out. So I just gave up on it and I let it go.

I lived the life of obesity for most of my life. I didn't know what it was like to be thin, or healthy for that matter. I never felt like a thin guy trapped in a fat body because I never knew what the whole concept of being thin was. That doesn't mean that I didn't look at other thin people and say, I wish I could be that way. I wish I could go to the movies and be able to fit into the seats. I wish that I could go to a 'normal' store and buy 'normal' sized clothes. I had those thoughts constantly and ironically, I grew content on being overweight because I feared how to be thin. Sounds silly I suppose.

I coped by convincing myself the world needs fat people too. It was my job and responsibility to be that fat person. I mean, I was really good at it. I had years of experience, I was jovial, had a good attitude, and I knew a bunch of other 'chubby' people who I called friends who allowed me to feel comfortable when I went out to social events. I had it all for being a fat guy. I knew where all the greasy pits were and where all the delicious food was. I knew the owners of these restaurants and I could walk in, sit down and BOOM! There's my cheese steak, fries, a side order of this and a side order of that and the occasional milkshake and I'm ready to rock-and-roll. There is this saying that I now live by that I would not have been able to understand the concept of it until it happened to me.

*"When the fear of not doing something exceeds the fear of doing it, you have no choice but to get it done."*

**Louis, 400 lbs**

My fear of not doing something exceeded the fear of doing it one particular, life-changing week. A routine doctor visit resulted in me being told I had less than ten years to live. I was twenty-five(25) years young!

The doctor shared I was one of the most unhealthy people to ever walk through his door and highly recommended I get gastric bypass surgery. Gastric bypass was one of the only options I had to extend my life. At this time the procedure was fairly new as a treatment. There was a high mortality ratio and there were numerous complications.

I was definitely fearful of gastric bypass surgery. I did not want to be put to sleep and never wake up. I remember taking all the brochures and information on the procedure and getting into my car, opening the glove box, stuffing all the papers inside it, and closing it thinking that I still had ten years to figure it out.

One day passed. Then two. Then three – never any more thought about having the surgery. Then I received a phone call that a very good friend of mine, Mike, collapsed at work and entered into a diabetic coma. When I showed up at the hospital, all his family was already there. They feared the worse. We spoke to the nurse and found out the diabetic coma triggered a devastating line of other problems and infections.

Doctors gave Mike less than 5% chance to live.

The reason for such a low survival diagnosis was because of his obesity. They had to use two hospital beds to support him and there were no surrounding hospitals equipped to handle the necessary procedures to improve his chances of survival.

The best chance Mike had was just that – 'a chance.' It was difficult being in a room surrounded by family members saying goodbye to their loved one before his time. Moreover, it is especially frustrating when you have so much you want to say yourself but you close it in.

I remember Mike's son sitting near the edge of the bed telling him that tomorrow he was going to do this and the next day he was going to do that. His son promised him that he'd talk to that girl he always said he should talk to. Right there he explained day-by-day, month-by-month, year-by-year outlining his whole life in front of his dying father. It was his way of saying goodbye.

What rocked my world was when Mike's son and I stepped into the elevator leaving that day. His son looked at me and asked with the clearest face, "So, are you coming over for dinner?"

I replied, "We've been friends for a long time and you are like a little brother to me. What you and your family are going through is a lot and I could only imagine the pain and confusion you must be going through. Please, you don't have to put on a show for me, you can use my shoulder to lean on."

He replied, "I don't have time for that as I am the man of the house now. So, I'll ask you again. Are you coming over for dinner?"

His comments struck me hard, deep in the gut. Seeing this thirteen year old assuming such responsibility at a young age and so quickly was mind blowing. I did not know how to respond and the thought of him anchored with me the entire ride home. I needed to talk with someone.

My best friend at that time, Joe, was someone who had an amazing gift in making any bad or negative situation into a positive one. He always looked at the glass as 'half full.' When he walked into a room people would light up from his charisma and energy would spread like wildfire. He was an amazing human being and also proud father of a new baby boy. Everyone needs a Joe in their life. I should note that Joe was also severely obese.

I visited Joe and I told him what happened with Mike. In moments Joe had me laughing and was doing what Joe does best - getting my mind off of things. I left Joe after a few hours and headed home. Shockingly, I was woken up by a phone call next morning with news that Joe had died of a heart attack in his sleep.

Another overweight friend checked off the list.

One might reasonably think that the combination of receiving a ten year death notice from my own obesity, having a best friend in ICU from complications resulting from obesity, and having another obese best friend die from sudden heart attack – all within a few days - that I would have had the greatest wake-up call ever.

Nope.

Maybe it was just being overwhelmed but it did not all sink in until I was at Joe's funeral. It was an open casket ceremony and it was time for me to pay my respect. I approached the casket and peered down inside. What I saw made the hair on the back of my neck stand up. Goosebumps covered my arms and I felt like the whole world shifted and spun around me. I felt trapped in a movie when I looked down and saw *myself* lying there, in a casket. It was as if I was looking into a mirror.

Talk about fear?

*That* was the day fear struck me right in my mind, body, and soul. I remember turning away, rubbing my eyes, looking back and still seeing myself lying in the casket. I never had an out-of-body experience before in my life nor do I ever want one again. It scared me so bad I immediately left the funeral.

I drove home as fast as I could and sat down on the edge of my bed, staring into the mirror. In that moment, fears from the past painfully surfaced. I remembered being picked on and tormented and how I used to hate going to school. I thought about how I couldn't even fly in a plane without upgrading to first class because I could not fit in coach. How I never went to the movies because the seats were too small. I thought about all the events I missed in life. I thought about the course of events that led up to where I was to that day, in that moment.

Then I began thinking about where I wanted to be when I got older and my future. I quickly realized that I did not want to leave a two month baby boy behind like Joe did – a baby that would never know his father. I did not want to be like Mike in a hospital with my friends and loved ones surrounding me, all wondering if I would make it through the night.

I became aggravated with myself. I thought, "Why did my friends have to be sacrificed for me to finally get the wake- up call and do something I was always fearful to do? To simply make a change?"

I sat there on the edge of my bed staring into the mirror in silence. I did not feel worthy to do anything else but sit there and face reality. I stared into that mirror until I passed out.

I woke up the next morning and immediately thought to myself, "Louis, this is the first day of your *new* life. Now is the time to change your lifestyle. Now is the time to change your relationship with food. Now is the time no longer be scared. Now the fear of not doing something has exceeded the fear of doing it and I have no choice but to get it done."

I set measurable goals for myself and I set visual goals as well. I drove to a popular clothing store and purchased an XL t-shirt and a size 38 pants. At the time I was a 5XL t-shirt and a size 56 pants! I put these new clothes on a hanger and hung them on my mirror as a daily empowering reminder of what would come. I sat there with my clothes hanging on the mirror, in my own reflection and I said, "This is it. This is your day and you will do this. And you will do it on your own because you caused this on your own. There are no shortcuts."

It took me two years, but I lost 207 pounds! I now weigh less than the weight I have lost. I am the healthiest I have ever been in my life and my doctor agrees. I became the thin guy that I never knew could exist.

*Louis, 180 lbs*

Now I can do everything I ever wanted to do and I am not afraid to do anything. I am not afraid to ask for a promotion. I am not afraid to ask for a date. I am not afraid of going out and being social. This is because the greatest fear in my life - the FEAR of CHANGE - was accomplished.

If I can accomplish my life's greatest fear then there is nothing in the world that could ever stop me. No challenge, roadblock, or barrier could ever stop me from doing what I now want to do. *That is the gratification and fulfillment you get from accomplishing your greatest fears.*

So the question I ask and counsel people on a day-to-day basis is, "What are you afraid of?" After we talk through their fear(s), I then ask, "Why are you afraid?" and we reflect upon their life and think about whether they have done, or are doing and what they really, truly desire. Perhaps it is that conversation, going on that trip, asking the boss for that promotion, jumping from that plane, traveling cross country, moving from their hometown, losing weight … you get the point.

Whatever the case is, think of something you are afraid of doing. Write that in the box below and do not continue until you envision what that is.

$$\Bigg[ \quad \textit{\underline{What am I afraid of}}\textit{?} \quad \Bigg]$$

Now that you have envisioned something you have been afraid of doing, I want you to ask yourself the following question:

$$\Bigg[ \quad \textit{\underline{What would your life be like NOT having this fear}}\textit{?} \quad \Bigg]$$

Would you be in a better place with it being done? If you answer, "Yes," or even if the possibility is "Maybe," then I ask, "Why are you NOT doing it?" You cannot allow the fear of *not* doing something exceed the fear of doing it any longer. Be a self-starter, go out there and squash your fears. Become a better person and someone in control of your life, your future, your destiny.

Do not hold back for both your sake and your friends and family. As human beings we were not meant to hold back. We are made to create beauty and empowerment in this universe. So go and achieve and do wonderful things. Just don't let fear stop you.

## About the Author

*Louis Vitiello, Jr.*

Louis Vitiello Jr. has achieved a level of personal health after an amazing life-changing journey. His unique approach of "simple steps to health and wellness" stems from self-taught lessons after losing over 200 pounds combine with his education from the Institute for Integrative Nutrition, the World's Largest Nutrition School. The Institute for Integrative Nutrition teaches over 100 dietary theories, practical lifestyle management techniques, and innovative coaching methods with some of the world's top health and wellness experts, such as; Dr. Andrew Weil, Dr. Deepak Chopra, Dr. David Katz, Dr. Walter Willet, Geneen Roth, and many other leading researchers and nutritional authorities.

When it comes to health coaching, Louis works with groups and individuals in face-to-face, on the Internet, or over the phone. He created the Simple Steps Weight Loss Program containing 'simple steps' one can integrated into their lives to help achieve a more balanced and healthy lifestyle. Louis believes that a program containing a health coach who will guide you on the right path of true health and wellness can be a major benefit to anyone serious about losing weight.

www.SimpleStepsWeightLoss.com

Louis@SimpleStepsWeightLoss.com

# THROUGH THE EYES OF A CHILD

*by Karen Alexander*

*"So what do we do? Anything. Something. So long as we just don't sit there. If we screw it up, start over. Try something else. If we wait until we've satisfied all the uncertainties, it may be too late."* ~ Lee Iacocca

What is stopping you from the next step? Are there walls between you and your success? Can you recognize the barriers that have been put around you? Do you know how to knock them down?

My past has had its own barriers and walls made of 'shoulds.'

Maybe you too have been 'should'ed' on. You know, you 'should' go to this school; you 'shouldn't' marry that man; you 'shouldn't' move to that city; this is how you 'should' raise your children.

I can definitely say that I have been 'should'ed' on many times, and perhaps maybe even I have 'should'ed' on a few people myself. In this ever progression of life knowledge, I am learning to no longer 'should' around my life and the lives of others.

My own son, Paul Jr. (PJ), inspired me with a lesson of breakthrough not too many years ago.

---

It was a difficult pregnancy and the cesarean was scheduled for 8:30 am on a Monday. The delightful day came and our 10 lb., 4 ounce baby boy was brought into our world. My husband and I immediately did the usual parental inspection…ten toes, ten fingers, deep dimples, a blazing crop of red hair and a big blue eye. Yes, just one big eye – the other appeared to be glued shut. The pediatrician patronizingly assured us that this was not uncommon and that PJ's eye 'should' open in just a day or two.

Unfortunately that did not happen. For my son's six week checkup I found a new pediatrician. Doctor #2 also had similar passive advice and said not to be concerned. Several months and several doctors passed.

Then at nine months old, PJ had a cold, runny nose, slight fever and was not sleeping. I made an appointment at a new doctor's office with Dr. Leventhal who had been highly recommended. The doctor examined PJ, looked up and pleasantly said, "Well I can certainly prescribe an antibiotic for the congestion, but what is wrong with his eye?"

Tears welled up in my eyes. I knew. Moms know when something is wrong. The next few weeks were the biggest whirl of neurosurgeons, CAT scans, MRI's, second opinions and insurance calls. The confirmed diagnosis: *Right Craniosynostosis*. It is even scarier than it sounds. The soft spot on the right side of the skull had prematurely sealed causing the skull to grow incorrectly, forcing the forehead down further and further over his left eye.

The most recommended neurosurgeon, Dr. Marzluff, had seen this only once before in his practice. He sat with my husband and me, calmly explaining the procedure as gently as possible. The operation would require an incision over the top of the skull from ear to ear. The skin would be peeled down. The bone would be separated and a piece of what looks like saran wrap would be placed at the skull seam to allow correct growth. Without the surgery there would be no less than severe retardation and brain damage, possibly blindness, and a very low chance of ... death. With the surgery, Dr. Marzluff continued to explain, because my son's fair skin, the bruising will look as if "I took your son by the feet and whacked him up against an oak tree."

The insurance had approved five days in intensive care and explained there 'should' be an additional two weeks in the hospital. Dr. Marzluff thought this 'should' be adequate.

Within weeks the cold steel doors of the operating room closed as we quietly prayed for the best and silently feared the worse. Minutes seemed like hours and finally the ordeal was over. My sedated son was brought to recovery. His innocent little body had more needles and monitors than you could imagine and a surgical turban encompassed his little head. Yet to everyone's surprise, there was not a bruise to be found. The doctor was cautiously optimistic and we allowed ourselves to feel just bit of relief.

After a long bedside night in intensive care, we were awoken by a familiar cry. PJ was hungry. The nurse asked what he normally eats for breakfast and brought us his tray. PJ was doing fabulous and moving so much that the nurses were somewhat uneasy. When the doctor came for the first follow up examination, he was astounded with the progress and said there was no need for the confinement of intensive care. Although it had been less than twenty four hours our baby patient was off to the pediatric floor.

The next day Dr. Leventhal came by to see his little patient. When he walked into the room, he was shocked to see our PJ standing up in the crib, still with two IV's, monitors, a surgical turban covering the 48 staples holding his incision together but also a big, dimpled grin and two bright beautiful blue eyes.

To everyone's surprised, he was released from the hospital in *days* not weeks. You see, while there was much malaise about the severity of the surgery for little PJ, we all forgot to tell *him*. Not one of us told my son what he 'shouldn't' do or how he 'should' feel. With full relief from his nine month headache, he was ready and raring to go!

As PJ grew, we carefully watched his progress. Although we did not allow him to play football, he enjoyed boy scouts, bikes, video games, music and much, much more. With the exception of a quarter inch scar over his head from ear to ear where no hair would grow, his development has been relatively uneventful, praise the Lord, and he has grown into a wonderful young man.

---

Through the eyes of this child, you can have your own relief from the pain and become raring to go. You do not have to listen to all that others 'should' on you. You can escape from the box of 'should's' you have been stuck in and realize your own limitless possibilities.

Know that you do have this incredible power within you. Please allow me to share a few examples of breaking through my own walls of 'should's'.

---

When I graduated high school in the 70's, I had been accepted at the University of Massachusetts, Amherst and at the College of Charleston in South Carolina. However, at that time those around gave me those old familiar 'should's' - you 'shouldn't' need that now; you are getting married and you 'should' be happy with that. After PJ's surgery, I decided to take *my own* advice. With a new sense of determination, I enrolled at Charleston Southern University to earn my bachelor's degree.

As a full time employee, the mother of two, and a full time accelerated evening student, I achieved my goal in less than 5 years. This would not have been possible without much appreciated help from my wonderful daughter, Nicole, and my 'wasband,' Paul. Both were present and proud as I walked the stage to receive my diploma in 1993.

---

I have worked in my chosen field of human resources for most of the 20 years that have followed. It has been my pleasure and personal reward to contribute to the positive growth of the organizations and the individuals on many occasions. I have been a part of recruiting and hiring hundreds, offering each a new opportunity to make a difference in their own chosen field.

Occasionally it was also necessary to allow certain staff members to find an opportunity elsewhere that more closely aligned with their own goals. I have welcomed and oriented, created a 'Cradle to Grave' supervisory training, developed programs which guided and assisted others to be the best they can be and as well as meet organizational needs and required goals. I know the details of payroll, benefits, compensation (oh yes, that's exciting!) and have guided numerous staff members through some difficult and complex decisions. I am known to be an advocate for the employee and have made numerous friends who have made their own difference in my life.

In this time, I have also been laid off, downsized, reorganized, eliminated, and yes, even fired. I know change. I know lessons learned.

---

At one of these junctures, I took a dramatic and delightful left turn. With a marriage that had failed and a generous severance package, I decided to fill yet another dream that had smoldered for countless years. I had learned to cook from my grandmother, Ethel, and my own father, Bryce Myers, Sr. I made my first wedding cake when I was 15 years old. I had catered to small and medium size functions with great success and delightful compliments as a sideline throughout my career. When I entertained in my home, accolades would abound.

Many of my friends and family told me I 'shouldn't' do this, 'shouldn't' take this risk, I 'should' invest this money or use it for something more conservative, more safe. I knew it was now or never. I broke through those 'should'y' walls and in January of 2004 I took what was a great risk, as well as a phenomenal, unquestionable reward, and began to form my business, Saguaro, LLC, dba the Carolina Café and Casual Catering. After the first year, my son, PJ, became my operating manager which was an added bonus to this adventure.

In the small town of Summerville, SC, I grew to be a local favorite. As the winner of the Chili Cook-Off and two Chocolate Festivals, customers often asked for my recipes. Mayan Omelets; Quiche Florentine; Chicken Salad Croissants; Broccoli Soup; Seafood Bisque; Jumbo Blueberry Muffins; and the Incredible Kiser Cake; just to share a few customer preferences. It was my true pleasure to serve, and from weddings to boxed lunches to 'Faye Trays' catering was an added bonus to this exciting endeavor.

It was a difficult decision but the right one, and after four years of personal and profitable success, I closed this chapter and sold my café. Carolina Cafe will always be the treasured memory of a dream fulfilled.

---

Now I am calling you to action. What walls are holding you in? What is it that someone or several have convinced you that you 'should' or 'should not' do? Break through these walls, say no to the 'nay sayer' and compartmentalize them into a delete folder.

Take that step now and see yourself soar!

## About the Author
*Karen Alexander*

Karen is a Senior Professional in Human Resources with over twenty years of experience primarily in the healthcare field. She earned her bachelor's degree in Business Administration from Charleston Southern University with a dual major in both Management and Economics and will be a 2014 MBA graduate from Wingate University in Hendersonville, NC.

Karen earned the highest educational award in Toastmasters International, Distinguished Toastmaster, in 1999. Through this membership she has won several speech contests and trained thousands through state opportunities. A servant leader who held the role of District Governor for District 58, South Carolina, 2000-2001, Karen led her team to the honor of Select Distinguished District with the rank of 14th in the world.

She is a volunteer with the local Hospice house and enjoys finding waterfalls in the mountains of western North Carolina. She is the mother of two; Nicole, and Paul Jr. (PJ); the mother-in-law of Danny, and the cool Grama of Meghan. Her best buddy is Charlie, her totally spoiled 14 year old black lab mix (he has his own room).

Karen brings together her experience and style to help you train and motivate audiences of all sizes and mixes. She can be reached at karenalexander28739@gmail.com or 843-509-7514.

# THE ANSWER LIES BEHIND THE NEXT DOOR

*by Neal Robert Anderson, J.D.*

*"Your success and significance in life will be in direct proportion to the number of times you put yourself (and others) in a situation to hear a yes...or a no."*
~ Neal Robert Anderson

I pulled my Jeep Cherokee off of Interstate 10, heading into the small central Texas town looking for the town hall to obtain a solicitor's permit for selling books door-to-door. It was a hot, dry Texas summer day. I drank a big gulp of water.

Approaching the railroad tracks, which had no crossing arms, I heard a train whistle and noticed a train coming from the North. After crossing the railroad tracks and seeing the town hall just ahead, I noticed a Saturn speeding towards me oblivious to the speed limit or the approaching train. I stuck my arm out of the window and motioned frantically for it to slow down. I looked in my rear view mirror and then turned around to see the train coming full steam ahead.

The car did not stop. SLAM!

The train hit the Saturn, sounding like a thousand tin cans being crushed at once as it was thrown a hundred yards down the tracks. I pulled into the town hall parking lot, climbed out of my Jeep, reached for my First Aid kit and froze. What had I just witnessed? My mouth tasted sour with fear. Were they all dead?

I saw an older gentleman wearing overalls jump out of his pickup truck and run to the crushed car. He climbed under the Saturn and began pulling two kids out. I ran up to the car and by this time there were several people standing around. The mother and her third son were pinned in the car. This family had been on their way to Six Flags in Dallas, Texas, when they met me on the road.

The firemen, police and EMT's tried for over an hour to get the mother and son out of the car. Finally, they were extricated and flown to the hospital, none of us knowing their fate. I still cannot believe I saw such destruction when before everything was normal. Lives changed in an instant. There was a large crowd. Many people speculated as to what had happened. After hearing several versions of how the events unfolded, I decided I needed to tell my story since I was the sole eyewitness. When the helicopter flew out of sight, I walked over to the town hall to give my account to the police. I'm sure you can imagine how an experience like this had and still has an effect on my soul.

I was living ten miles south in Temple, Texas, for the summer. My hometown was in Bloomington, Indiana, and I was in my second year in the Southwestern Company's summer internship program. College students across the country go to Nashville, Tennessee, for a week of sales and leadership school and then go to a different part of the country to find their own place to live, get up at 6am every morning, take ice cold showers, then go door to door for 14 hours, 6 days per week, working on straight commission, and paying their own expenses. Students make anywhere from $8,000 on the low end to over $100,000 in a summer. There are no guarantees. My team was selling in the Austin, Texas, region and I was assigned to the school districts surrounding Temple. Anyone that has sold door-to-door knows that rejection is par for the course and being 2,000 miles away from home can cause even the toughest people to experience a little homesickness!

By the time the investigator invited me inside his truck to give my account, it was already 11:30 am. I began telling him about me crossing the tracks and hearing the train whistle. While I was recounting the accident my emotions began to overtake me. What happened to the mom and son? Did the other two children live? This could have been me had I traveled up Highway 10 just one mile an hour slower. Crash. I froze. I had almost finished my story when the investigator informed me that his batteries had died and I needed to recount the accident again.

Could this be happening? Part of me wanted to go home. Was this all a dream?

Now it was just before 1 pm and I had a goal of doing 30 demonstrations per day and I had done one. I was five hours behind and getting 30 demonstrations done in 14 hours is difficult enough, but I had just witnessed the most frightening and traumatic event of my life. Maybe I could pack it in for the day. I had a valid excuse. "Take the day off, Neal. You have witnessed more than you should have to see. Half the day is gone. Just go home."

But I couldn't go home. There are two types of people in this world: ones who look for a way and the others who look for an excuse. Too often people make excuses for their lot in life. They blame other people instead of taking responsibility for themselves. I must admit I was very tempted to call it a day. The emotional energy required to sell is only known by those who do it for a living. Now, picture you have to go door-to-door, face your fears, get doors slammed in your face, be called names, and you have to do this for the next nine hours. I had not seen my family or friends in a month. Thank God I am a person who finds a way.

Just before leaving the investigator's truck I asked him, "Sir, I have this crazy summer job where we go out 14 hours per day and sell these really cool homework manuals to families who notice that school is a bit different since they were in school and the parents want to have something around the house to help save time with homework and relieve frustration. I committed to myself and to others that I would do 30 demonstrations per day. It's 1 pm and I have done one demo. I'm five hours behind so I'm wondering. Do you have kids in school?"

The investigator replied, "Yes, and as a matter of fact, my son needs a lot of help in school."

I ran to my car and pulled out my sample case. I grabbed one of the handbooks and showed him the section that had all of the formulas for geometry on two pages. He was impressed. I simply said, "Here is what everyone likes about the way we do business: we take orders today and then I deliver them right before school and give the kids a quick lesson on how to use them. If you were to get a set that would help for the new school year, wouldn't it?"

I learned in our training that the answer is always 'no' if you do not ask. I likely first learned that concept around age four. I had nothing to lose. I knew this person cared about his son and wanted him to have the best shot at doing well in school. I also knew that my product could help. The investigator signed the order.

It was now 1:15 pm and I had two demonstrations and 28 to go. Some people find a way...other people find excuses. I was determined to find a way.

I thanked the investigator for helping his son and began talking to myself. "I can, I will, I'm going to help 30 families today live a richer, fuller, more meaningful life because I stopped by and showed them my books. I need a call, I need a demo, and I need a sale and I need all three to have a good day, 'who's next?' I'm not a doctor and I'm not a family therapist so all I can do right now is go out and simply work my butt off and help families have the materials to help their kids. Who's next?"

*How* we talk to ourselves makes all the difference.

I drove past the town hall and took a right on the first street I could find. I pulled into the driveway, grabbed my sample case, and ran up to the door. "This is going to be the coolest family I meet all day. They are going to love these books." I rehearsed my approach in my head and the mom agreed to visiting with me. I quickly discovered that this woman was the algebra teacher at the local high school.

I told her the story of what I had just witnessed and she told me to gaze across the street. That was the Bulls' house—the home of the family who was fighting for their lives. The math teacher bought a set of my books and gave me a few referrals. This was the first door that I knocked on in this new school district in Troy. Your success rate goes way up if you have teachers who have purchased your books.

This teacher praised my efforts and thanked me for stopping by. Three demonstrations down, 27 to go.

The answer lies behind the next door.

Before I left I gave the math teacher a set of books for the Bulls. I did not know if they would live, but I was counting on it and was not sure if I would still be in the area when they were released from the hospital. I was more than willing to donate a set of books to a family that was going through so much.

I continued to knock on doors. I ran between houses. And for the next eight and a half hours I heard plenty of no's and some yes's. By the time the clock struck 10pm I had accomplished 34 demonstrations (four more than my goal) and 10 customers for one of my best sales days ever. But more importantly, I was able to help a lot of families get books that would help their children. I was able to take a tragic situation and focus on what I could control. And I was able to keep going when most people have told me they would have quit. I made almost $700, which was a lot of money considering I paid my own way through college.

I clearly remember driving home with a heavy heart for the Bulls' family, but a huge smile for doing my best with the cards I was dealt. I found a way when an excuse was so easy to find and use. I had the opportunity to take a somewhat crazy situation and find the silver lining. What would you do? Do you quit too early?

I ended up selling books for four more summers and meeting tens of thousands more families. It was amazing to discover that every answer I sought was behind the next door - all I had to do was knock.

A few weeks after the Bull's accident, I approached a mobile home. A mom was sitting on a picnic table outside and a man was just entering the mobile home. I got out of my Jeep and ran up to the mom. "Hey, I'm Neal, I'm the one who has been sitting down with all the families in the area." I noticed tears streaming down the mom's face.

"What's the matter, ma'am?" I asked.

Her reply would develop a passion I did not know I had. "Did you see that man that just went inside? He just asked me for a divorce. And he has all the money and all of the lawyers and he will take everything."

My heart sank. This poor mom was scared to death that she would be left out in the cold (even in Texas). She felt helpless. I prayed with her and ran back to my Jeep. I remember saying to myself that this is never going to happen again. I was going to law school no matter what.

I finished that summer in the top 30 out of over 3,000 sales people. I also returned to school that fall with 45 credit hours needed for graduation and decided that I wanted to enter law school the following fall. That meant I would have to take 23 credit hours one semester and 22 the next. Full time is 12-15 credit hours and I was recruiting and leading a group of students at Indiana University, so extra time was not something that I felt I had. However, I knew that I could find a way.

I ended up taking 23 credit hours in the fall and 22 hours in the spring, graduating a semester early and accomplishing my goal of entering law school in the fall.

Had I not knocked on that door and experienced the situation with that mom on the picnic table, I likely would not have realized I had a passion for what a law degree could do to help people who felt helpless. Had I not continued to work that day in Troy, Texas, I would have been a day behind, which means I would not have met the mom at the picnic table at that exact moment that her husband notified her of a pending divorce. This event was the catalyst for me to go to law school. And in order to pay for law school I had to continue to work with Southwestern three more summers.

At the end of the next summer before entering law school, I met an attractive, charming, southern girl at the company headquarters just after receiving my check for an entire summer of work. I turned to the leader of the organization and said, "Well, time to go pay for my first year of law school." Somehow this statement made an impression on this girl and we ended up officially meeting a few months later in the Houston airport on our way to the company's incentive trip to Puerta Vallarta over Thanksgiving vacation. This began a friendship that developed into something much more. Who would have known back on the picnic table that I was putting the pieces together that would lead to this girl being my wife...who has given me three beautiful boys.

I have my wife and my boys because I was willing to make a cold call on a woman who just learned that her husband wanted a divorce. Knocking on one more door when you feel like quitting is when you know that something good is about to happen right around the corner.

Unfortunately, people quit too early and often blame their circumstances on others instead of themselves. They wait for passion rather than acting their way into feeling passionate. Passion follows effort every time. It may appear to be a passion, but unless you have done the hard work of becoming an expert, you probably are not seeing all of the struggles involved. Remember, the grass is brown on both sides of the fence. It's your attitude that waters and fertilizes it to turn green - or turn brown.

I faced wanting to quit thousands of times. Thankfully I learned that there were only two things that I could control: my attitude and my work habits. Too often people fail to take responsibility for not only their actions but also their inaction. It's easier to blame our circumstances rather than realizing that it is our thinking and inaction that causes fear and failure. It may feel a lot more comfortable in the short term to make excuses, but the excuses catch up to us. Eventually we have to take responsibility for how we choose to react to situations.

This is one point in my life that my decision to act changed not only my life but has served as an example to help hundreds of others believe that they too can push a little harder and knock on one more door. The yes's pay the bills; the no's build the character. Too often people find the no's too painful and quit before they ever get a chance at getting a yes. Wanting to quit is OK. Quitting is not.

Over the course of my college summers with my door-to-door sales job, I struggled, I had joy, I cried, and I laughed, I met funny people, I met mean people, I met weird people, I met smelly people, I met cool people. I met rich people and poor people. I had flat tires; a pit bull chased me. I was soaking wet, and I was hot. I was able to see life happening to thousands of people and more importantly being able to see how they reacted to it in real time. As Charlie 'Tremendous' Jones, a motivational author says, "You are the same person five years from now except for the people you meet and the books you read." Meeting tens of thousands of people from across their threshold has taught me not only a ton about myself but what makes people tick - and also why many don't.

A week rarely goes by without someone asking me to tell them about my experience selling books door-to-door. It's amazing what you learn about people sitting down with them in their living room on their terms. People act a little differently when they cross their threshold and head out into the world. People often put on the mask and do things at home they would never do outside the home. Fortunately, I was able to catch people right in the middle of life. And then I got to interview them for 14 hours a day for six summers. I've been in Tennessee, North Carolina, Texas, Oklahoma, Pennsylvania, Ohio, Alabama, Mississippi, Missouri and Nebraska. I've visited with hundreds of teachers and principals, factory workers, lawyers, doctors, bait shop owners and the unemployed. One thing is for sure; people are generally good and people are pretty much the same regardless of territory. It's funny how people are usually a reflection of *you*.

I had been delivering my books to my Troy customers at the end of that summer after witnessing the accident. Several customers mentioned that Zach, age 12, and Bernice Bulls were home from the hospital recovering. They had lived. These same people, some of whom who were related to the Bulls, told me I should stop by and meet them. The Bulls wanted to personally thank me for saving their lives.

I did not want to draw attention to myself. As I was delivering books to the Bulls' subdivision (their house was on the corner at the entrance to the subdivision so I passed their house numerous times over a two-day period but did not stop), I ran into yet another mom who said I should stop by and meet the Bulls on my way out of town. I wasn't sure if I should. After pulling to the stop sign at the corner for the last time getting ready to turn left to leave town, I decided to turn around. I parked next to their mailbox and knocked on the glass door to their modest home.

I saw a woman sitting in a wheelchair through the sliding glass door. Mr. Bulls opened the door and when he saw my Jeep he knew right away who I was. I said, "It's great to meet you." He turned around and yelled into the house, "Hey, come meet the man who saved your lives." Zach and their other kids came into the room.

As Zach entered the room I could tell he had come a long way in his recovery even though he still had bruises on his face 6 weeks later. This was a very touching moment. I remember Mr. Bulls being shaken up when he reached the accident scene. I can only imagine what he went through on the way to the hospital and then helping his wife and son recover. Here I was in their living room hearing him thank me for saving their lives. All I did was motion for them to slow down. Experts said this simple act slowed them down just enough so the train didn't hit them broadside and at full force. We visited for a few more minutes and I left. My summer in Troy, Texas, was officially over.

Fast forward three summers. I was at the company headquarters in Nashville, Tennessee, settling my account at the end of my fifth summer working in Southwestern's program. I was ready to begin my third year of law school. A student approached me and asked, "Are you Neal Anderson?" I replied I was and he said, "I met Mrs. Bulls in Texas. She said you saved her life and she bought a few books from me that completed the set of books that you gave her four years ago."

I was speechless. Here was a person who had been assigned the same sales territory as I had been four years before. What are the chances that he would find Mrs. Bulls house and catch her at home? What are the chances that we would both be in Nashville at the same time as everyone has different check out dates? The answer indeed lies behind the next door and thankfully this young man knocked on the Bull's door.

We will never know how our lives could have turned out differently if we didn't face our fears and make a decision to make difficult choices and act on those choices even when it might not make sense at the time. When you are knocked down what will you do? What are the doors upon which you need to knock? Will you knock on one more door when you feel like no one is buying? I can't promise that the answer to *all* of your questions in life can be answered, but one thing is for sure: if you don't knock you will never know.

*"Your passion will be in direct proportion to the effort you are exerting and the sacrifices you are willing to make."*
*~ Neal Robert Anderson*

## About the Author

*Neal Robert Anderson, J.D.*

Neal is an inspirational speaker, consultant and performance coach with a passion for helping individuals and companies increase significance and profitability. Neal is an expert at getting to the emotional difference that people make in other people's lives, and has designed retreats that get people out of the office and on a sailboat or the Appalachian Trail, the Adirondack Mountains, or the Intracoastal Waterway. His clients include everyone from a 2-time Super Bowl Champion to hundreds of top-producing sales leaders across the country.

He has conducted over 50,000 one on one sales interviews (over half of which were door to door), performed thousands of sales presentations and has helped people get to places they never thought possible in their personal and professional lives. By unplugging, Neal believes you can strip away the "poser" self and can get to the core of who you are and the difference you can make in other people's lives.

Neal was a competitive ski racer graduating from an elite New England Ski Racing Prep School, earned an undergraduate degree from Indiana University, where he studied under Hall of Fame Coach Bobby Knight, and received a law degree from Vermont Law School.

Neal lives in Raleigh, North Carolina with his awesome wife, 3 energetic and dynamic boys and has a vision of changing the world.

neal@adirondackadventurecompany.com
www.adirondackadventurecompany.com

# STEP OUT OF MEDIOCRITY & INTO YOUR GREATNESS!

*by Dexter L. Scott*

*"If at the end of each day we haven't challenged our own mediocrity, we are destined to repeat a cycle of complacency."*
~ Dexter L. Scott

I have a few questions for you:

Have you ever felt, with 100% certainty, that there was more for you to offer but you were caught in a system of mediocrity?

Have you ever followed a dream and realized you may have made a mistake? Perhaps gone down the wrong path at some point?

If you have, then we have something in common. Hopefully, my story will resonate with you and cause you to identify things that have been holding you back. I am extremely honored to share my story with you in hopes that it will **EMPOWER** you to flee from mediocrity and step into your **GREATNESS**. And, here's my story...

## MY JOURNEY

After graduating from college in 1995, I moved to Raleigh in search of the perfect job. I had a Business Management Degree in hand with the Latin phrase in mind, 'Carpe Diem,' which means 'Seize the Day.'

My job search was initially challenging but I ended up landing a rewarding banking position. I had the opportunity to learn how the lending world worked; however, I soon realized that sitting behind a desk was not my forte. I needed a quick change. In April of 2000, I began working for the State of North Carolina. I was appointed as a State Bank Examiner for the North Carolina Office of the Commissioner of Banks (NCCOB). I traveled 100% of the time across the state and country to various conferences – there was no desk to sit behind in this position! The job was rewarding but it still did not fulfill my inner desire to make a difference.

I married my beautiful wife in 2001. Being away from her and home for numerous amounts of time was not what I wanted to continue doing. I worked for NCCOB until May of 2005 before transitioning to the North Carolina Department of Administration as a Compliance Specialist. I thought I had found a specific employment direction and this was my big opportunity – wow, I was soon in for an awakening! As I settled into this new position, I quickly realized that it also had its limitations. I came to find out that this system would literally cripple my creativity to grow and develop. Allow me to give you a snapshot of my timeline during the week:

## MONDAY

Parking my vehicle in the parking deck, I would strut down the walkway ready to begin a fresh week of work. I called myself 'Mr. Perpetual Optimism' as former General Colin Powell said in one of his quotes. The walkway was packed with government employees headed to their respective offices. As I would greet them in the morning, I rarely received a reply, and if I did, it was half-hearted. People did not seem enthusiastic or engaged. As I walked into the elevator, I would exchange an occasional smile and acknowledgment. Once I arrived to the office, things would get a little better. The work day began.

## TUESDAY

The atmosphere walking from the parking deck lightened up a bit. The people seemed to be a bit more jovial, a bit more relaxed. The needed smiles, the good morning responses, the "How was your weekend?" all made for a somewhat inviting atmosphere. The work day began.

## WEDNESDAY

People on the elevator are talking about their weekend plans and where they are going for lunch. You would think this was an entirely different place! Smiles flowing, people speaking, and the entire atmosphere lifted. 'Hump Day' was great only because people were looking forward to the weekend. The work day finally began.

## THURSDAY

I cannot believe what I am experiencing. The entire government complex is different and provides an atmosphere that anyone would want to work in. Everyone is speaking and laughter fills the hallway from different departments. The work day finally, finally began.

## FRIDAY

I am at a loss for words. Productivity has gone down tremendously. People seemed to float instead of walk. The atmosphere was charged with excitement only due to the weekend plans and getting home - it's *'PARTY TIME!' I am not even sure the work day began.*

**The cycle begins all over again the following Monday morning.**

For 78 weeks, this was my life. I quickly realized that this 'patterned system' was robotically engrained and would never change. From Monday to Friday, the same atmosphere, the same behavior, the same anticipation for the weekend, this same routine caused me to move backwards in my growth. I was not engaging life and I failed to challenge my mediocrity. Over this period of time, I read maybe two books (not to completion I might add).

I became a part of the environment in which I was experiencing. I ran into a lot of good people who walked the hallways. People who managed the environment the best they could. You could tell there was something in them that they wanted to get out, they wanted to explore, they wanted to move to a greater scale. Sadly though, this environment did not provide that opportunity. I wondered how many people settled for this and how many people gave up on their dreams for this so called stable environment. This was not my reality and I felt destined to accomplish more.

### ENOUGH ALREADY – TIME TO STEP OUT!

In 2005, my wife and I refinanced our home. I had an impromptu conversation with the appraiser for our home. Longing to make some type of professional change and grow from mediocrity, I asked our appraiser questions about his work and being a business owner. I researched more about the appraisal business and within two months was enrolled in Real Estate Appraisal School. For the next three years, I studied under three(3) Certified Appraisers and appraised over 500 homes.

I felt it was my time to step out and soon resigned my position from the government, withdrew my retirement, and I began to chart my course to success. I was well on my way ... or at least I thought.

In 2008, I was prepared to launch out and guess what happened? The market crashed and the housing bubble burst! Appraisers were stripped of long time relationships with loan officers they had developed for years. Most appraisers had to reduce their fee to stay afloat which destroyed the appraisal profession for newcomers. I did not know which way to turn or in which direction to go. I was completely dismayed and lost to say the least.

## THE 'AMAKENING' OF GREATNESS

During this very challenging time in my life, my wife and I were introduced to a network marketing business through my brother and sister-in-law. This business was fairly new to *us* but it was rapidly gaining in popularity. We got involved, with my wife taking the helm, and quickly shot up the ladder hitting one level from the top amassing $100,000 in only 4 months! Things were great and through this avenue, my greatness was revealed. Talk about timing…this couldn't have worked out better.

Due to our success, my wife and I, along with other achievers, were invited to attend the company extravaganza in Las Vegas. Over 3,000 people throughout the country gathered to get pumped up, gain insight into the industry and be introduced to the company's top performers. After a brief intermission, the emcee announced the next guest coming up to the stage.

When the music started and the person walked on stage, I was completely blown away. It was Mr. Les Brown! I watched this man on YouTube hundreds of times and there he was standing right in front of me. I was mesmerized by his message and how he seemingly spoke directly to me. He called forth what was in me, something that I had known deep down inside for some time.

After his presentation, I ran from the ballroom of the MGM Grand all the way up to Mr. Brown's room and fearlessly met him face to face. From that meeting, I was chosen to be in the 1st Empowerment Mentoring Group held by Les Brown and Paul Martinelli. For one entire year, I was trained and taught by the best. This training allowed me to look back into my childhood and realize that I had always felt a magnetic attraction to become a speaker. In school, I had a natural knack for communication. I reflected on my college experience when I presented in front of class and it was seamless to get into the flow of communicating. *This*, speaking, was truly the path in which I needed to walk! Thinking about my previous jobs, I further came to the realization that I always gravitated towards the communicating elements of any position. The speaker in me had been born.

**GREATNESS PUT INTO ACTION**

After this year of training in the Empowerment Mentoring Group, my mindset changed and my consciousness shifted to pursue my **GREATNESS**. I immediately began to call myself, 'International Motivational Speaker' as I envisioned my speaking to be worldwide. There wasn't any sense of playing it small. I recall one of Les Brown's quotes that always fire's me up:

> "Shoot for the moon because if you miss you will land among the stars." ~ Les Brown

As I spoke it, I believed it. I increased my level of learning by reading several books including:

- *Think and Grow Rich* ~ Napoleon Hill
- *Your Invisible Power* ~ Genevieve Behrend
- *Get Paid for Who You Are* ~ David Wood
- *As a Man Thinketh* ~ James Allen
- *Psycho Cybernetics* ~ Dr. Maxwell Maltz

**TIME TO PUT THE GREATNESS TO WORK**

As I marketed myself as a speaker and picked up a few gigs, I was always on the lookout for other opportunities. As I was searching through a job site one day, I came across a posting that would change my life **FOREVER** and launch me into my **GREATNESS**. The requirements of the position were for the candidate to learn and present an eight page script, record it on video and send it in within one week to the company headquarters. I was prepared, I was ready and I was relentless in my pursuit for **GREATNESS**. I memorized the script, found the perfect place to record the presentation and gave it my all.

Within days of the submission, I received a phone call to present before a panel in the National Office. I was flown across the country and presented before a panel of five senior managers. Although I was nervous, I felt deep within that this was God's hand upon my direction. Days later, I was offered the position. My dreams came true and continue to grow further as I now travel up and down the east coast speaking to thousands of families each year. Not to mention my declaration of becoming an 'International Motivational Speaker' has also become a reality. My job has afforded me the opportunity to speak with students in Australia, New Zealand and Europe.

**MY INDIVIDUAL GREATNESS REVEALED**

The more I speak, the more I come alive. There's another quote that I have developed from my experiences:

*"Always remain in the pursuit of BECOMING because if you ever catch yourself, you might slip into mediocrity."* - Unlocking the SEAL to EMPOWER YOU ~ Dexter L. Scott

You will notice I end my quotes with the phrase, 'Unlocking the SEAL to EMPOWER YOU.' One day while I was contemplating my blessings and journey, I recalled the process of canning from observing my mom growing up. I would be fascinated by watching her 'can' preserves. The process of canning is not that difficult. The contents placed in the can are done so by the creator and at the appropriate time, the **SEAL** is broken and the contents revealed.

I feel that it is my calling to 'Unlock the **SEAL** that **EMPOWERS**.' Working for the government I watched many people being controlled by a system that did not serve or advance their creativity. I believe many of these people had become 'canned.' They had contents within them that just needed to be unlocked. For many of them, their dreams had been forgotten, their desires to become more had been depleted. Only until someone 'UNLOCKED' that potential could they get beyond a place of mediocrity.

While I have been enjoying the opportunity to travel and speak as a career, I have also developed a message that will help people **STEP OUT OF MEDIOCRITY AND INTO THEIR GREATNESS.** From my experiences, I have broken down the steps that will help anyone ready to leave their mediocrity behind and move into their **GREATNESS.**

# The S.E.A.L. Process

## S – STRATEGY

What is your strategy for success? You must have steps in place in order to make strides toward stepping into your **GREATNESS**. The following quote addresses strategy:

> *"Most people don't plan to fail; they fail to plan."*
> ~ John L. Beckley

When I decided to become a professional speaker, I relentlessly pursued this passion. My strategy was to study various speakers such as Les Brown, Paul Martinelli, Zig Ziglar, Tony Robbins, Jim Rohn, and many others on an hourly basis. I began to practice several hours a week to become the best, to be the best and to maximize my stage presence.

## E – EDUCATE YOURSELF

When you decide on the direction of your **GREATNESS**, you have to immerse yourself into learning all that you can about it.

> *"Education is the most powerful weapon you can use to change the world."* ~ Nelson Mandela

As a speaker, true spontaneity can only come when you have mastered your subject matter. When I speak on a topic, I ensure I know more than what I am asked to speak about. What about your topic? How much have you immersed yourself into it to make sure you know it like the back of your hand?

So what constitutes being an expert? It requires 320 hours to be considered an expert in celebrity gossip and 42,240 to become a Neurosurgeon. Using these 2 extremes and dividing them by two, I believe you will need somewhere in the average of 21,280 hours to be considered an expert in your field. I have always considered 25,000 as a benchmark for myself. Whatever the number, I will never stop learning and growing and I trust you feel the same way, despite the research given us.

**A – ACTION**

You MUST take action. In order to manifest your **GREATNESS**, action is a requirement.

> *"When you advance confidently in the direction of your dreams, and endeavor to live the life you have imagined, you will meet with a success, unexpected, in common hours."* ~ Henry David Thoreau

Situations and circumstances do not have to be perfect in order for you to take action. As a matter of fact, situations and circumstances WILL NEVER be perfect. You will encounter obstacles but you must use these as stepping stones to advance forward. When I decided to become a speaker, I was not a member of any reputable organizations such as the NSA (National Speakers Association) or Toastmasters. I simply made the decision to speak and opportunities resulted.

I recall heading out of town and passing by a non-profit organization when the thought instantly hit me that they may need my assistance. I picked up my cell phone, made a phone call and it resulted into a series of leadership and public speaking workshops. Had I not made the call, nothing would have happened. It's about action and having the guts to move.

Think about a spider for one moment. Have you ever walked outside and saw a spider web from one tree to the next and wondered how it happened? Spiders have a very unique ability to transport themselves. As a matter of fact, spiders have been known to be seen 30,000 feet in the air by pilots flying commercial airlines. Spiders have also been seen by sailors far from land getting caught in the ship sails. When a spider decides to take action, he turns his body around toward the wind, releases its silk and through the process of ballooning, the spider heads towards unchartered territory. Wherever the wind blows the spider goes. Spiders do not spend hours thinking about it, they don't ponder its significance, they don't worry - they just take action. If a spider can take action, so can you! Taking action will open up doors for you that you would never imagine possible. Opportunities are never lost, they are just passed along to someone else.

**L – LIFE LONG LEARNING**

Dedicate yourself to being a life-long learner. At the point you stop increasing, you start decreasing. During my years of being in the 'system', I lost complete focus and the drive to become more … to be more! When I began to live my dreams, my desire to learn became more like a flame of fire.

> *"He who learns but does not think, is lost! He who thinks but does not learn is in great danger"*
> ~ Confucius

I listed some of the books I read in the previous section to help me learn and grow. Just the thought of not increasing gives me chills. My journey prior to stepping into my **GREATNESS** served its purpose. It taught me valuable lessons. It taught me lessons that otherwise I would not have learned. I am constantly looking to grow and learn about various things to continually improve as a speaker. I listen to, at a minimum, 10 hours of motivational messages each week via YouTube, Ted Talk and various other sources. I read articles and clippings of things to enlighten me and push me further. I attend seminars. I am constantly looking for ways to invest in my personal growth and development. Basically, it is a never-ending passion pursuit for me and should be for you as well!

> *"When the end comes for you, let it find you climbing a new mountain instead of slipping down an old one."*
> ~ Jim Rohn

**CHAPTER DEDICATION**

This chapter is dedicated to my father, **Wilbur Scott**. He passed away at the age of 65 on June 9th, 2011 from pancreatic cancer which is intentionally lowercased because I DO NOT wish to give it power over anyone reading this. I was hired in my position in May of 2011 and my father stayed alive long enough to hear my

**GREATNESS** being put into action. When I returned from my flight across country, I was able to tell him all about it and he was happy and excited for me. Shortly afterward, his health rapidly decreased until he departed this earth.

What is amazing is the timing of it all. Upon being hired, I needed to get my passport for my flight to Australia and New Zealand while dealing with my father's health. I was not going to take an international flight with my father in the hospital fighting for his life. My father passed away on Thursday June 9th, we buried him on Wednesday June 15th, I was on my way to Washington, DC on Friday June 17th to get an emergency passport and on Sunday June 19th, I was on an 18 hour flight to New Zealand.

As I have looked back on this journey so many times, I know that the chain of events have strengthened me to continue onward.

To my father, **Wilbur Scott**, I owe the tenacity, relentlessness and the dedication to be the man he raised me to be and to never settle for anything that looks like mediocrity.

To **OUR GREATNESS**...

## About the Author

*Dexter L. Scott*

Dexter L. Scott is the Head of Admissions for *People to People Ambassador Programs* for the states of Maryland, North Carolina, Virginia, West Virginia and the Washington, D.C. area. He works with over 2,000 families and over 200 teacher leaders each year presenting programs that take students to all seven(7) continents. Dexter has spoken to more than 20,000 people in the last three years, both nationally and internationally, in Australia, New Zealand and Europe.

Dexter believes in stepping out of mediocrity into **GREATNESS** and by doing so, phenomenal things can happen as identified in many of his stories such as staying in the exact same hotel as the President of the United States in 2012. You should hear him tell this story! Dexter is married to his lovely wife Tonya and they have four children, Tailiah, Kiera, Morgan and Tyler and they currently live in Rolesville, NC.

Reach Dexter at dexter@dexterlscott.com

# The Crossroads

*by Jean A. Sturgill*

*... For unto whomsoever much is given, of him shall be much required ...*
*~ Luke 12:48*

It was June 2007. I was standing in the street looking at a photo album that belonged to a street minister who I had met that day. As I flipped through the pages, he stood there with me. My eyes landed on a photo that was taken the previous year in Daytona of the word "JESUS" written in the sky.

As tears began to roll down my face, I stood there completely speechless.

The street minister tried to console me, but he had no way of knowing what I was feeling. He tried to lighten things up by saying, "If I'd known it was going to make you cry, I wouldn't have shown it to you!"

As I reached out toward the photo, he commented that the tears were tears of love. He was right.

In an instant, I had been reminded of the day that I saw the word "JESUS" written in the sky over 10 years prior when I was on my way to see my parents in Henderson, North Carolina. Had a skywriter created it? Or, was it a miracle in cloud formation? Either way, I had found encouragement.

The road between these two events had been full of both personal and business challenges - good and bad. The journey had drawn me closer to God.

In 1997, my dad had a stroke. After that, he wasn't quite himself. The strong opinionated man who I had come to lean on for advice was suddenly much less outspoken. Two years later, he passed away. God had been there for me every step of the way; He began to fill the role of father to me - the fatherless (Psa 68:5).

In 2000, Bob, my husband, had returned from a business trip with the idea that our boys should have a website. Robbie and Drew said they wanted to reach the world for Jesus, and we started looking into building DrewsAnimals.com. Again, God provided!

In 2001, we celebrated the launch of our new website, but it was quickly overshadowed by the death of the only grandmother I had ever known. Later that year, Bob became unemployed when the company he worked for went bankrupt. Again, God provided. However, we found ourselves living in two states for the next 13 months, and we were separated by an almost five hour drive. I struggled with it initially, but God showed me that this was His will for our lives. What could have been a nightmare became a blessing in so many ways. Since we homeschooled, we had the time and the flexibility to travel the roads. We saw a lot of Washington, D.C., and I had a haven to work on Drew's Animals.

2003 – 2006 brought business adventures. In one case, I went to New Orleans after Katrina had blown through. God placed it on my heart to check the room reservation before I got on the plane. As it turned out, the room was not available after all. Rooms were hard to find, but God provided again.

At the end of 2006, I felt led to give up a position that I held in a business organization. I had learned a lot about leadership, and I'd done a lot of speaking. It was now time to move on. I still had the business that I had started years before, and I felt like it needed to grow in another direction. I just wasn't really sure what that was.

A few months later, in March 2007, God placed it on my heart to write a book - *Bouncing Beaver Discovers God*. I had actually written a version of this book a couple of years back, but - except for the scripture in it - the book was horrible. God provided a new title, and I knew I'd have to start over.

Now it was June, and my family (and team) had come with me to this rough neighborhood to participate in a street ministry event. Although we had the Drew's Animals products to sell, the real focus was on giving out New Testaments and getting the neighborhood children to draw pictures for us to put on the website. Our hope was that they would be able to visit our website to see the photos and encounter scripture in the process. We wanted to be a witness and a blessing both then and later.

Did I mention that this was a rough neighborhood? When we first drove up, I think it was assumed that we were lost. We probably looked a little out of place. It was definitely not a neighborhood that my father would have considered safe. Had he been living, he would have been concerned. Of course, he would have been concerned over that Katrina thing too. In both cases, I was merely following what I felt that God had for me that day.

I had not anticipated encountering a photo that would take me back across 10+ years of my life during which God had been so faithful. It was like I had come face to face with Him in an instant, and the tears poured down.

This was a God encounter like no other God encounter that I'd ever had. This was a loud and clear answer to the months old question, "What am I supposed to be doing with Drew's Animals?" This was a moment in time when I knew that I was standing exactly where God wanted me to stand, and I was doing exactly what God wanted me to be doing. I don't believe in coincidences, and seeing this photo carried a message into the depths of my heart that God cares specifically about me. He is a personal God in every sense and in more ways than I had ever imagined. I was completely overwhelmed with emotion and completely speechless. God had spoken up!!

Over the years, it had been moments like this - where I followed God, and He answered - that grew my faith. Every good leader believes in himself or herself. I fall short at times. I make up for it by believing God and trusting in His provision. Along the way, He has taught me lessons in leadership - directly and sometimes through others - of courage, truth, and love. Now, it was time to apply what I had learned.

**HAVE COURAGE**

In the fall of 2007, after time on my knees in prayer, God gave me my first book - *Bouncing Beaver Discovers God*. I thought it would be a nice gesture to give some copies to the library. I thought that all I needed to do was to drop them off. I was mistaken.

My first effort resulted in the book being returned to me without a proper review. My second effort resulted in my book being returned to me with a letter of rejection. The book was turned down for many reasons. One reason had to do with the book promoting a website. Another reason had to do with the library already having books with similar content.

I promptly showed the rejection letter to someone standing near me at the post office. Not knowing the plot, he suggested that I rewrite the book.

This wasn't going to happen because I wrote the story as I felt that God had given it to me. Besides that, Bouncing Beaver is a character on the Drew's Animals website. If I removed the mention of the website from whence she springs, mentions on several occasions as if it were a real physical place, and later returns, a huge part of the storyline would be missing. If I removed what I felt was being referred to as content similar to other books they already had, that would remove most of the rest of the book.

I was faced with two options. I could tear this short 10-minute read into shreds by trying to make it into someone else's vision - and a completely different book. Or, I could believe God - and believe in myself - and let it be. I found it easy to believe God, and I chose the latter.

I also chose to believe God when He told me that He did not need to teach me to be a speaker in order for me to have a children's ministry. I took that to mean that Drew's Animals was a beginning not an end to this journey.

Question: If we always change to please someone else, how many times is a "someone else" going to come along? We could chase that forever. Great leaders have courage. Believe God, and believe in yourself.

**WALK IN TRUTH**

The following year, 2008, I was praying for another children's book. One day my prayer request went up as something like, "Couldn't you just drop another book on my head?" The response came back, "I gave you a book." God had indeed provided. I just had not realized it until now. I'd been so focused on a children's book, and this wasn't going to be a children's book.

*You Are Who God Says You Are: 8 Steps to Overcoming the Past* was put on paper in about two months time. As a matter of fact, God opened the door for me to moderate a women's ministry using the book or the materials for the book if it wasn't finished by the time the ministry started. Over the next two years, I saw God work via that book.

Notice that I said this book was put on paper in about two months? God had been writing it in my heart for much longer.

Who am I? That's a question that I spent about 20 years trying to figure out. All the really bad emotionally scarring stuff was prior to 1988. I was still toting the burden in 2007 until God healed it.

I had been so messed up for so long that I was not even aware of all the ways that it was marking my life.

We each walk in our own reality. It's not always the truth, but it is what we believe.

The condensed version of the story is that the mud puddle of sin splashed on me, and somewhere along the way I started to splash it on others. As for the initial mud puddle, that was not my fault. However, the decade of bad decisions that followed was my fault. Although I had been saved at an early age, and I should have avoided much of this, I didn't.

Pain stemming from my past continually held me back. I was once asked to do a self-evaluation of my job performance. It might sound silly, but I cried for three days over an evaluation form that should have taken 5 minutes to fill out.

I had a real battle going on inside. I believed so many lies about myself. There was no way I was comfortable giving myself high marks on this form. I did not feel deserving. In reality, I had worked very hard. I had earned high marks in many areas. The scale was 1 to 5, and no number seemed right. Certainly I did not deserve a 1 or a 2, but I did not feel that I had earned a 4 or 5. A 3 would be failing, and I did not feel that was true either.

I was frustrated with myself. On and on the battle went inside of me until I found the courage to walk in the truth supported by facts. It was then that I was able to give myself a 4 or 5 when I had earned it.

Why the drama? As we go through life, we tend to adopt as truth the things that others say to us verbally, what we read into their actions, and the things that we tell ourselves. Many of these things are lies. When lies and bad things get tangled together, they emerge as fears and become scars of the past.

Fear affects our self-image and our relationships. That touches every personal and professional area of our life.

"For God hath not given us the spirit of fear; but of power, and of love, and of a sound mind." (2 Timothy 1:7)

God spent a long time showing me the truth about me. In November 2007, He had taken the pain of my past away. My past no longer held me in chains. It was time to write the book, and it was time to help others overcome.

Each day, I face a choice. I can choose to believe lies and walk in fear (from the Greek - faithlessness), or I can believe the truth and walk in power, love, and a sound mind. I make an effort to choose the latter.

You face a choice too. Great leaders walk in truth. What will you choose?

**LOVE OTHERS**

In 2009, God had placed it on my heart to go by a certain radio station and give them five copies of my latest book. I also thought about offering a one-minute thought for the day. Although I knew the lady at the station, the time had never seemed right to make those offers.

Christmas was nearing, and the phone rang. It was the radio station, and I was asked if I'd come do an interview that night. I would be the only guest that evening. By the time I left we'd given away the five books, and she had asked me to do a radio segment that would run five or six days a week.

The *Realizing Your Winning Potential* segment ran on that station for about 2 years, and it was also played sporadically during the second year on another station that could be heard in six counties and surrounding areas in eastern North Carolina. The written version was posted as blog entries on my website - YourWinningPotential.com. I granted permission in August 2013 for it to air again in the future via an Internet radio station.

It's one way God chose to show His love for others through me. I'm not taking any real credit here. I simply walked in obedience through the doors God opened, and I showed up with a pen and a prayer as needed.

How do you show your love for others or let God show His love for others through you? Great leaders strive to love others unconditionally. It shows in how they give back.

**YOUR CHALLENGE**

If you had told me 10 years ago that I would write multiple books, be on the radio, and speak to groups on both Christian and business topics, I'd have laughed. I'd have told you that I did not like to write. I'd have talked about the book that I started, but never finished. I'd have also said that I wasn't sure about hearing my own voice on the radio. I'd have made excuses about not being able to create enough content for a regular radio segment.

I challenge you to walk like a great leader. Have courage. Walk in truth, and strive to love others unconditionally. I also challenge you to always walk by faith (2 Co 5:7).

It's AMAZING what happens when God steps in!!

# About the Author

*Jean Sturgill*

Jean A. Sturgill speaks to both the Christian and the secular market. Her seminars and workshops focus on a range of topics from leadership, management, and business ethics to growing your relationship with the Lord.

Over the years, Jean has held many leadership roles including Area Director for BNI, and Toastmasters Area Governor in District 37. She most recently earned her DTM (Distinguished Toastmaster award).

Jean's radio segment, *Realizing Your Winning Potential*, aired for about 2 years. She's the author of multiple books, and her writing has been published in *Alamance Magazine*. Visit YourWinningPotential.com for more information.

# MY BIG PROMOTION:
## *Finding Opportunities Hidden Behind Life's Challenges*

*by Dauv Evans, Ph.D.*

Have you ever received a promotion before? Take a moment to reflect on how you felt after receiving that promotion. You were probably excited and felt a sense of accomplishment. But, have you ever received a promotion that made you feel inferior or made you question your own abilities? That's how I felt when I was thrown into my big promotion. Most of us hold preconceived notions, formulated by society, of what constitutes economic and career success. I was among the many professionals who placed a disproportionate amount of value on my career, measuring my success according to position, pay, and prestige. Not only did my last promotion help me redefine my career, but it also enabled me to learn how to find the opportunities hidden behind life's challenges.

## My Promotion

2012 was an eventful year for me, to say the least. I got married, my first child was born (a son), I was on the cusp of completing my doctoral program, and I moved from Raleigh, North Carolina to Nashville, Tennessee for a promotion. Once in Nashville, I seldom saw my new wife and son because so much of my time was monopolized by my new job. My job required me to do three main things. I was usually taking calls at all times of the day and night, attending endless meetings, and holding consultations with other employees. I was good at my job and received positive feedback on my performance. I enjoyed the process of rolling out new initiatives for the organization and helping those initiatives become successful. I justified the time away from my family by convincing myself that it was normal and inevitable. The amount of time and energy I put into my career was necessary to sustain our standard of living, I told myself. I liked what I did, but I did not yet realize how much it was jeopardizing my family relationships.

  For years, I had aspirations of starting my own consulting and speaking business. I enjoyed working with people one-on-one and speaking to large audiences. I was passionate about starting my own business, and yet there always seemed to be one more milestone that I had to reach before I embarked on my new enterprise. I would say to my wife, "I'll start my business after the wedding," or "maybe when I finish school." Once I reached those milestones, I would tell her, "I'll get started when I save little more money," or "wait until work dies down." I always had another obligation that served as an excuse for waiting just a little longer to start my own business. One day while at work, I received an email from HR stating they wanted to talk to me personally about a new initiative. I was excited about working on a new project, and I was anticipating the accolades I would be getting about my recent performance. The next morning, I was contacted by the HR representative for our scheduled appointment, and I found out that I would not in fact be working on the new initiative. Even worse, instead of telling me how good of a job I was doing, the HR representative told me that I now had *no job*. It turns out that the organization I worked for was downsizing, and I was being laid off. Have you ever been faced with a challenge like this?

**My Big Promotion**

When I got home to my wife and told her the awful news, she took it well. Her positive attitude was not contagious, however. I had just uprooted my new family to a city where we didn't know anyone else and had no support network, and now I was without employment. This was the first time I had not had a job since I graduated college, so this was a new experience for me. It was devastating, and it quelled any hubris I might have had. Yet when I thought about it, now that work was no longer consuming my time, I had more time to start the business that I had put off for so long. I suddenly felt like there was a little ray of hope in the midst of my gloomy situation. I immediately began working on a business plan for my new enterprise.

Within days of receiving the news that I had been laid off, I was already in the process of turning my negative situation into an opportunity--or so I thought. It turns out my wife had a little news for me.

She came home one afternoon and said, "Sweetie lumpkins, I've got some good news for you. I was offered a new career opportunity back in Raleigh."

To which I replied, "Well that's great, honey; it looks like we're moving back to Raleigh." I knew there had to be more because when my wife begins any sentence with "sweetie lumpkins," it can't be good.

"You've been promoted!" she continued enthusiastically.

"Promoted, to what?" I replied.

She explained, "You have been promoted to professional infant technician."

I was puzzled.

After a pause, she said, "You have been promoted to...an au pair extraordinaire."

Again, I was perplexed. An au pair sounded like some kind of fruit chef. Then my wife said, frustrated, "You'll be a stay-at-home dad."

The first thought that ran across my mind was that she must be joking. Once I figured out that she was quite serious, the shock set in. I could not imagine being at home by myself for eight or more hours with an infant. I was terrified and had a sinking feeling that my entrepreneurial aspirations would be postponed for months, if not years. A few weeks later, she started training for her new job, which meant that my own on-the-job training would begin simultaneously. Working with my most demanding client, my four-month-old son, kept me busy and required three main duties.

First, I answered when he called, day and night. Sometimes

for something to eat, other times for a hug, on special occasions he just needed to remind me of what his "duty" was. Second, we had endless meetings from the time he got up in the morning, until he went to bed at night. The meetings usually consisted of reading motivational literature authored by Dr. Seuss and singing our A-B-Cs. Third, I conducted one-on-one consultation sessions with my son via facetime. Not the facetime synonymous with apple products, but the old school facetime; you may know it by the term "peek-a-boo." The little free time I did have was spent recovering from sleep deprivation.

How could I possibly start a business when my time is monopolized with my son and house chores? I thought I was off to an inauspicious start since my new job was devoid of any tasks resembling consulting or public speaking.

**Opportunity behind Life's Challenges**

I knew that if things continued along these lines, I would continue to be unhappy and resent myself for not making the most of my situation. Something had to give, but what? I couldn't make an organization hire me. Someone had to stay home to take care of my son. I needed time to start a business. These were all variables that I had limited control over. I did, however, have control over my mindset and the way I viewed my situation.

I learned that the significant challenges we face are in reality the major turning points in our lives. The way we perceive our situation determines the positive or negative course of our lives. The day I changed my perspective was the day I accepted my situation and realized that it was replete with opportunities. This realization got me thinking: how many people miss opportunities because they're not thinking outside the box or because life is not going exactly how they had imagined it would? In the midst of this economic downturn, people may think that there is a lack of opportunities. On the contrary, challenges present the greatest opportunities. My challenging situation taught me the value of time, taught me why I should embrace change, and taught me the necessity of reordering my priorities in life.

**Ph.Done.**

When I was working full-time, I was limited to working on my dissertation on occasional nights and weekends. I was constantly going back and forth with my committee to make the necessary corrections and defend my argument. This was a cumbersome and time-consuming process. Receiving feedback from my committee confirming that I had adequately addressed a committee member's concerns took weeks. I was also adjusting to my new job at home, so I spent a lot of time learning my new role, which sometimes spilled over into my personal time. This meant even less time to work on my dissertation.

By the time I made the transition to being a stay-at-home dad, I still had the looming challenge of completing my Ph.D. Although I was closer to finishing at that point, the dissertation was arguably the most difficult part of my program. Once I changed my perspective, though, my big promotion gave me the opportunity to complete my Ph.D. program more quickly. After I became more proficient with my new job duties as a stay-at-home dad, I became more efficient with my time. My son's sleeping schedule became increasingly predictable, which allowed me to plan around it. I would write and conduct research around his nap and feeding times. I was able to address my committee members' concerns much more efficiently, which enabled me to move through the process much more rapidly than before.

The continuous progress culminated in the completion of my program. I finally received my Ph.D. after exactly five years, to the month. With school out of the way, I now had a little more free time and a lot of momentum.

My 'promotion' taught me how to take advantage and maximize my time. It was amazing what I could get done in just an hour or two here and there throughout the day when I adhered to a plan. My plan outlined the small tasks that I wanted to accomplish during each break. I learned that I could maximize my time by making a plan. A plan eliminates the guesswork in accomplishing your goal and enables you to be more efficient.

Achieving milestones regularly can build momentum and reinforce a work ethic that is more conducive to being consistently productive. Are you missing out on an opportunity to be more productive in reaching your goals?

**The Business of Change**

Attaining a significant goal like my Ph.D. motivated me to pursue even more challenging goals. When I was working full-time, I had allowed just about any obstacle to prevent me from starting my own speaking and consulting business. Between work and school, I had little time to work on my own business. Although I was satisfied with my full-time job, it was not my passion. So those long days really weighed down on me and left me too drained to work on any 'extracurricular' activities. But I was also in my comfort zone. I had a decent position, with reasonable hours, and more than adequate pay; I was too comfortable to invest time, money, and energy in a risky venture. The lack of any support made it even more difficult since my wife and I didn't know anyone in Nashville, where we were living.

My new position as a stay-at-home 'professional infant technician' kept me busy. Still, despite my hectic schedule, I had little pockets of free time throughout the day to work on outside interests. My previous position had restricted me to working on these projects during some nights and weekends. I found that I now had time to work on my consulting business if I planned ahead as well as I had for school. My consulting business presented a unique challenge because unlike school, starting a business was a relatively unstructured project. Nevertheless, I found time to outline my business plan and clarify my goals.

I created a list of milestones and corresponding resources that could assist me in achieving each milestone. I found convenient times to volunteer and join social groups, which helped me to build new connections with other professionals of my ilk. My newfound free time allowed me to practice my crafts—speaking and consulting—on a semi-regular basis. I identified people who were either currently doing what I wanted to do or were, like myself, in the process of establishing themselves. I was able to practice my other passion, teaching, regularly, now that my schedule was more flexible. As my wife's schedule became more flexible as well, I was able to do more to grow my consulting business. Although we had not had a support system in Nashville, our move back to Raleigh afforded us the opportunity of being surrounded by our old network. I had more contacts in Raleigh than in Nashville, as well as two sets of grandparents who could help watch our son on occasion.

I stated earlier that my big promotion at first made me feel inadequate and question my own abilities. Essentially, my new role made me uncomfortable, and that was actually the best thing that could have happened to me. I learned to embrace being uncomfortable: not to wallow in it, but to use it to promote my professional development.

Think about the challenging situations in your past that you have persevered through. How much have you grown by learning, adapting, and persevering through those uncomfortable changes?

**Family Man**

Completing my Ph.D. program and starting my own business was satisfying to me, but neither of those goals was nearly as important as getting to spend more quality time with my family. I worked between 40 and 50 hours per week for the job that had brought me to Nashville. Sometimes my job required me to travel, and I worked on a handful of projects at home. As with any new position, I wanted to ensure I learned my job as quickly as possible, so I spent extra time in training and using my personal time to better understand my role. I would usually work an eight or nine hour day. If I was teaching a course that evening I would work a twelve hour day. Once I added my academic obligations to my work schedule, I was left with very little time for my family. Most evenings when I got home, my son was either in bed for the evening or getting ready for bed. Even though I was on diaper, feeding, and night duty on the weekends, I still missed out on a lot those first few months of his life.

After the big promotion, my family life changed significantly for the better. I was on night duty with my son almost every night. I learned all of the nursery rhymes and read to him each night. We took more time as a family to explore Nashville before we left. I was able to catch some of the little moments that I had missed when I was working a full-time job.

My wife and son became my new, most demanding clients. Suddenly, the focus was not on pay, position, accolades, scheduling, teleconferences, trainings, or even promotions. My focus was my family. At the end of the day, when my previous organization was done with my service, my family was right there to support me. I learned how important it is to reassess every now and again. It is so easy to get caught up in chasing after the shiny rewards our society has made synonymous with success. This was a new opportunity to redefine success.

How do you define success in life?

**The Takeaway**

While I was chasing the proverbial brass ring, I lost focus of what was truly important in life. Because of my limited perspective on my situation, I also had a challenging time identifying the opportunities right in front of me. My big promotion did not initially come with a salary increase or a fancy office, but there were plenty of rewards awaiting once I reassessed my priorities.

My promotion initially seemed like a demotion, but now I have the opportunity to spend time with my family and build a career that I'm passionate about. I had to reconstruct my previous views on success and on how to make it a reality.

What about you? What personal or professional challenges are you currently facing? What opportunities might be hidden behind that challenging situation? I have learned that opportunities are everywhere, especially in the midst of challenging situations. The most successful people are skilled at identifying opportunities. The next time you are confronted with an obstacle that makes you feel inferior and question your own abilities, I challenge you to identify the opportunities because it just might be your next promotion.

> *"Success is to be measured not so much by the position that one has reached in life as by the obstacles he has overcome."* ~ Booker T. Washington

## About the Author

*Dauv Evans, Ph.D.*

Dauv is the Founder of Keen Advisors, LLC which specializes in personal and professional development. His background is in higher education and corporate training. Dauv earned a Ph.D. in Leadership in Higher Education from Capella University.

Dauv holds an MBA from University of Phoenix and a B.A. in History from the University of North Carolina at Greensboro. He also teaches undergraduate business and U.S History. Dauv enjoys traveling the country sharing his story to help others become better at life. He wants others to be successful with overcoming the "how" by finding the opportunities in the 'now.'

Email: devans@dauvevans.com
Website: www.dauvevans.com

# CLOSING THOUGHTS

*by Dr. Kevin C. Snyder*

---

*How to Create the Circumstances You Want!*

I recently received a call from a friend, Sarah, whom I had unfortunately lost touch with since my move to North Carolina from Florida. She called to thank me for helping her vision a goal that had just manifested in her life.

Last year, Sarah's company hosted a competition where they were awarding an all-expenses-paid trip to Paris for the top earning account executive and their guest. Sarah, being one of the youngest and newest members of the team, also had an incredibly diligent work ethic and passionate drive for her work. And most importantly, she believed and had faith she could win that trip to Paris if she worked hard enough. She had VISION and GRIT.

When Sarah told me about the competition, I observed the conviction in her eyes and the hunger to win that award. She truly did envision going to Paris on the company's dime rather than just 'hope' to win and travel there. Sarah understood the difference between hoping something would happen and creating the circumstances in life to make it happen.

---

*Some people in life make things happen,
others watch things happen,
and some unfortunately wonder,
'What just happened?'*

---

So when Sarah told me about this exciting opportunity and asked for suggestions, I recommended to her that she think of a creative way to be reminded of and visualize winning that trip to Paris. Meaning, I wanted her to find a symbolic way to envision Paris each and every day until it manifested for her.

Sarah and I lost touch after that conversation due to the fact that I moved several states away. To be honest, I completely forgot about our Paris conversation and never followed up with her to hear the outcome.

When Sarah recently called me though, here's how the conversation about Paris transpired:

"Kevin," she said. "Do you remember that conversation we had about Paris last year and how badly I wanted to win that trip from my company?"

"Oh yeah, I sure do," I replied. "What ever happened?"

"Well," she said. "I just got back from Paris! I took my brother on the trip and it was phenomenal!"

"That is fantastic! Congratulations! I'm so proud of you." I said.

She continued, "I'm calling to thank you for helping me win that award. You made it possible and helped me believe in that dream coming to reality. Thank you."

"What are you talking about Sarah? You did all the work. I just had a conversation with you about it over a year ago."

"But you helped me vision it and that's why I won," she said. "If it were not for your idea to find that daily reminder of winning, I don't think I would have been as motivated. It was on my mind every day and helped me believe I deserved to win. So thank you!'

"Well," I replied. "I defer all credit back to you, but thank you for believing in the visualization process. It's powerful isn't it? I'm so happy for you Sarah."

Sarah and I continued our conversation for several more minutes and she shared details about what specifically she did to remind her of Paris on a daily basis. Unbeknownst to me until that conversation, Sarah took two significant actions which led to her ultimate success winning that trip to Paris. The first being that she created a goal board, commonly known as a vision board, with a list of all her goals and expectations she desired to come to fruition that year. She took clippings and pictures from magazines, typed and printed off her own phrases, and even put tangible symbols of items and pinned them to a piece of cork board. One of those items on her board was a picture of the Eiffel Tower with a typed phrase underneath reading, 'Congratulations, You Won the Trip To Paris!' Her vision board was that simple and took her only two hours to create.

The second vital action she took was buying a mini, one-inch Eiffel Tower key chain. Like her vision board, this figurative key chain was a symbolic, hourly reminder of not just Paris but more importantly winning her company's award. She knew she could travel to Paris at any time, but she wanted the satisfaction and fulfillment knowing it was an award from her company. Therefore, each time she grasped her keys to travel from appointment to appointment she would see that Eiffel Tower and be reminded about working even harder to win Paris.

---

*You must see your goals clearly and specifically <u>before</u> you can set out for them.*
*Hold them in your mind until they become second nature.*
*- Les Brown*

---

It is critically important to acknowledge that Sarah also worked diligently hard and was extremely persistent to win that Paris award. She also possessed an internal belief system which allowed her to believe she could beat the more experienced competition. But according to Sarah, what helped her most was visualizing Paris as a goal already achieved through her vision board and key chain. Those two symbols of achievement helped her to daydream with a purpose and activate her creative power of what I call 'intentional realization'. Quite simply, Sarah saw Paris not as what it could be, but as what it would be. She created and visualized the circumstances she wanted.

How often do you visualize goals like Sarah? When is the last time you allowed yourself to confidently daydream about a desire manifesting in your life? What is an exciting achievement you hope might someday happen but you never have done anything about it yet? If you are waiting for the ideal circumstance, how's that working for you?

Unfortunately for most of us, it has been a long time since we have allowed ourselves the creative freedom to listen to our hearts desires. We aspire for and envy significant accomplishments but we do not feel deserving of having such wonderful achievement. And with a seemingly lofty goal where we honestly have no clue where to start, we settle for never taking any action. Furthermore, we convince ourselves that circumstances need to be more ideal before we make any important decisions. As a result, we never fully experience the magnitude of greatness that exists in our lives and in the lives of others.

Leaders take action. Extraordinary leaders feel the fear and do it anyway. <u>They create the circumstances they want and expect</u>. You have read about many of them in this book.

So stop being *destructive* to yourself. I give you permission right now to only be creatively *constructive*. Identify a goal that has always been a 'What If?' in your life and start visualizing it in your life. You deserve it. Do what Sarah did and take time to create a vision board and find a symbol that can serve as a daily reminder for what will come, not what might come. If you don't do it, who will? As I have shared in previous column issues, the best way to do something is to start doing it. Achievement and greatness like never before are waiting for you to believe and act.

---

*Imagination is the preview to life's coming attractions.*
*~ Einstein*

---

THANK YOU for reading this book. Your investment in yourself has already proven valuable and we are honored to be part of your journey. If any of the authors can assist you with being your coach or cheerleader, please feel free to contact them.

To Your Continued Success and PASSION,

Dr. Kevin Snyder, Co-Editor, Speaker, Author
www.InspirActiveSolutions.com
Kevin@InspirActiveSolutions.com

# SUBMIT A CHAPTER FOR A FUTURE BOOK!

Everyone has a 'story' and <u>we want yours</u>! We are always looking for inspirational, true stories focused on leadership, accomplishment and heart-warming sacrifice for future issues of *Leading The Way*. Stories should be filled with such intense emotion that it captivates each reader and inspires them to live more fulfilled, intentional, and passionate life.

Authoring a book is an intense experience that requires countless hours of focused thought, disciplined writing, and repetitive editing. Many people have aspired to write a book – however, becoming an author is an accomplishment very few have ever achieved. Being published as a contributing author in future 'Leading The Way' projects will add further credibility to not only your resume vitae and professional experiences, but also to your personal fulfillment. All we need from you is your 'story.'

This is your opportunity to become a published author by submitting a chapter of content in lieu of hundreds of pages. Practically everyone I have encountered with a goal for authoring a book has never completed their dream because of one OR more combinations of these four (4) reasons: (1) not enough content to publish a full book, (2) too expensive, (3) they were quickly frustrated and confused by the hundreds of book publishers making false promises, and/or most commonly (4) they did not know how or even where to begin.

Authoring and publishing a book can be extremely difficult. The majority of work comes after the manuscript is written! The advantage to being involved with a future *Leading The Way* group project will be that you will become an acclaimed author with credibility and product to market yourself and/or sell! In addition, the powerful concept of a group book is that other authors on the project will be marketing you wherever their books travel as well. The exposure and marketing for you is literally exponential and limitless! You will never know where these books travel and who will notice you as an author.

How you sell, market, and give away your books is your complete discretion! Use your books as 'thank-you's' for clients and those you have conducted business with, sell online during/after speaking events, gift as holiday and birthday items, or give as mementos for close friends and family. Regardless of who receives your book, they will be impressed with your product and persistence to see it through completion!

For more information about deadline dates, chapter parameters, etc., contact: Kevin@InspirActiveSolutions.com.

# ABOUT THE AUTHORS

## Louis Vitiello, Jr.

Louis Vitiello Jr. has achieved a level of personal health after an amazing life-changing journey. His unique approach of "simple steps to health and wellness" stems from self-taught lessons after losing over 200 pounds combine with his education from the Institute for Integrative Nutrition, the World's Largest Nutrition School.

The Institute for Integrative Nutrition teaches over 100 dietary theories, practical lifestyle management techniques, and innovative coaching methods with some of the world's top health and wellness experts, such as; Dr. Andrew Weil, Dr. Deepak Chopra, Dr. David Katz, Dr. Walter Willet, Geneen Roth, and many other leading researchers and nutritional authorities.

When it comes to health coaching, Louis works with groups and individuals in face-to-face, on the Internet, or over the phone. He created the Simple Steps Weight Loss Program containing 'simple steps' one can integrated into their lives to help achieve a more balanced and healthy lifestyle. Louis believes that a program containing a health coach who will guide you on the right path of true health and wellness can be a major benefit to anyone serious about losing weight.   www.SimpleStepsWeightLoss.com

Louis@SimpleStepsWeightLoss.com

## *Karen Alexander*

Karen is a Senior Professional in Human Resources with over twenty years of experience primarily in the healthcare field. She earned her bachelor's degree in Business Administration from Charleston Southern University with a dual major in both Management and Economics and will be a 2014 MBA graduate from Wingate University in Hendersonville, NC.

Karen earned the highest educational award in Toastmasters International, Distinguished Toastmaster, in 1999. Through this membership she has won several speech contests and trained thousands through state opportunities. A servant leader who held the role of District Governor for District 58, South Carolina, 2000-2001, Karen led her team to the honor of Select Distinguished District with the rank of 14th in the world.

She is a volunteer with the local Hospice house and enjoys finding waterfalls in the mountains of western North Carolina. She is the mother of two; Nicole, and Paul Jr. (PJ); the mother-in-law of Danny, and the cool Grama of Meghan. Her best buddy is Charlie, her totally spoiled 14 year old black lab mix (he has his own room).

Karen brings together her experience and style to help you train and motivate audiences of all sizes and mixes. She can be reached at karenalexander28739@gmail.com.

## *Neal Robert Anderson, J.D.*

Neal is an inspirational speaker, consultant and performance coach with a passion for helping individuals and companies increase significance and profitability. Neal is an expert at getting to the emotional difference that people make in other people's lives, and has designed retreats that get people out of the office and on a sailboat or the Appalachian Trail, the Adirondack Mountains, or the Intracoastal Waterway. His clients include everyone from a 2-time Super Bowl Champion to hundreds of top-producing sales leaders across the country.

He has conducted over 50,000 one on one sales interviews (over half of which were door to door), performed thousands of sales presentations and has helped people get to places they never thought possible in their personal and professional lives. By unplugging, Neal believes you can strip away the "poser" self and can get to the core of who you are and the difference you can make in other people's lives.

Neal was a competitive ski racer graduating from an elite New England Ski Racing Prep School, earned an undergraduate degree from Indiana University, where he studied under Hall of Fame Coach Bobby Knight, and received a law degree from Vermont Law School.

Neal lives in Raleigh, North Carolina with his awesome wife, 3 energetic and dynamic boys, and has a vision of changing the world. through helping people realize their true calling.

neal@adirondackadventurecompany.com

## *Dexter L. Scott*

Dexter L. Scott is the Head of Admissions for *People to People Ambassador Programs* for the states of Maryland, North Carolina, Virginia, West Virginia and the Washington, D.C. area. He works with over 2,000 families and over 200 teacher leaders each year presenting programs that take students to all seven(7) continents. Dexter has spoken to more than 20,000 people in the last three years, both nationally and internationally, in Australia, New Zealand and Europe.

Dexter believes in stepping out of mediocrity into **GREATNESS** and by doing so, phenomenal things can happen as identified in many of his stories such as staying in the exact same hotel as the President of the United States in 2012. You should hear him tell this story! Dexter is married to his lovely wife Tonya and they have four children, Tailiah, Kiera, Morgan and Tyler and they currently live in Rolesville, NC.

Reach Dexter at dexter@dexterlscott.com

## *Jean Sturgill*

Jean A. Sturgill speaks to both the Christian and the secular market. Her seminars and workshops focus on a range of topics from leadership, management, and business ethics to growing your relationship with the Lord.

Over the years, Jean has held many leadership roles including Area Director for BNI, and Toastmasters Area Governor in District 37. She most recently earned her DTM (Distinguished Toastmaster award).

Jean's radio segment, *Realizing Your Winning Potential*, aired for about 2 years. She's the author of multiple books, and her writing has been published in *Alamance Magazine*. Visit www.YourWinningPotential.com for more information.

## *Dauv Evans, Ph.D.*

Dauv is the Founder of Keen Advisors, LLC which specializes in personal and professional development. His background is in higher education and corporate training. Dauv earned a Ph.D. in Leadership in Higher Education from Capella University.

He also holds an MBA from University of Phoenix and a B.A. in History from the University of North Carolina at Greensboro. He also teaches undergraduate business and U.S History. Dauv enjoys traveling the country sharing his story to help others become better at life. He wants others to be successful with overcoming the "how" by finding the opportunities in the 'now.'

Email: devans@dauvevans.com
Website: www.dauvevans.com

## Dr. Kevin C. Snyder

Dr. Kevin Snyder is a motivational speaker and author who has written six(6) books and keynoted over 850 motivational presentations in all 50 states. He has a passion for helping individuals develop a strategy to achieve their fullest potential and his specialty is in coaching aspiring authors and speakers get PAID to write and speak! He is also a certified skydiver and scuba diver, a sailing enthusiast, a musician and vocalist, and most importantly, a winner on the game show **'The Price is Right!'**

Kevin is an adjunct faculty member with the Center for Creative Leadership (CCL) which is the global leader in executive education and training. His speakers bureau, Inspir-ACTIVE Solutions, specializes in developing custom-based keynotes and leadership development seminars to ignite employee motivation, satisfaction, workforce performance and enhanced bottom-line results. If your company or association ever seeks a dynamic keynote speaker, then consider Inspir-Active Solutions!

Kevin earned his Doctorate in Educational Leadership from the University of Central Florida, a Masters in Educational Administration from the University of South Carolina and a Bachelor's in Marine Biology from the University of North Carolina at Wilmington. Contact him at:

www.InspirActiveSolutions.com

Kevin@InspirActiveSolutions.com

# LEAD THE WAY!

Made in the USA
Charleston, SC
05 September 2014